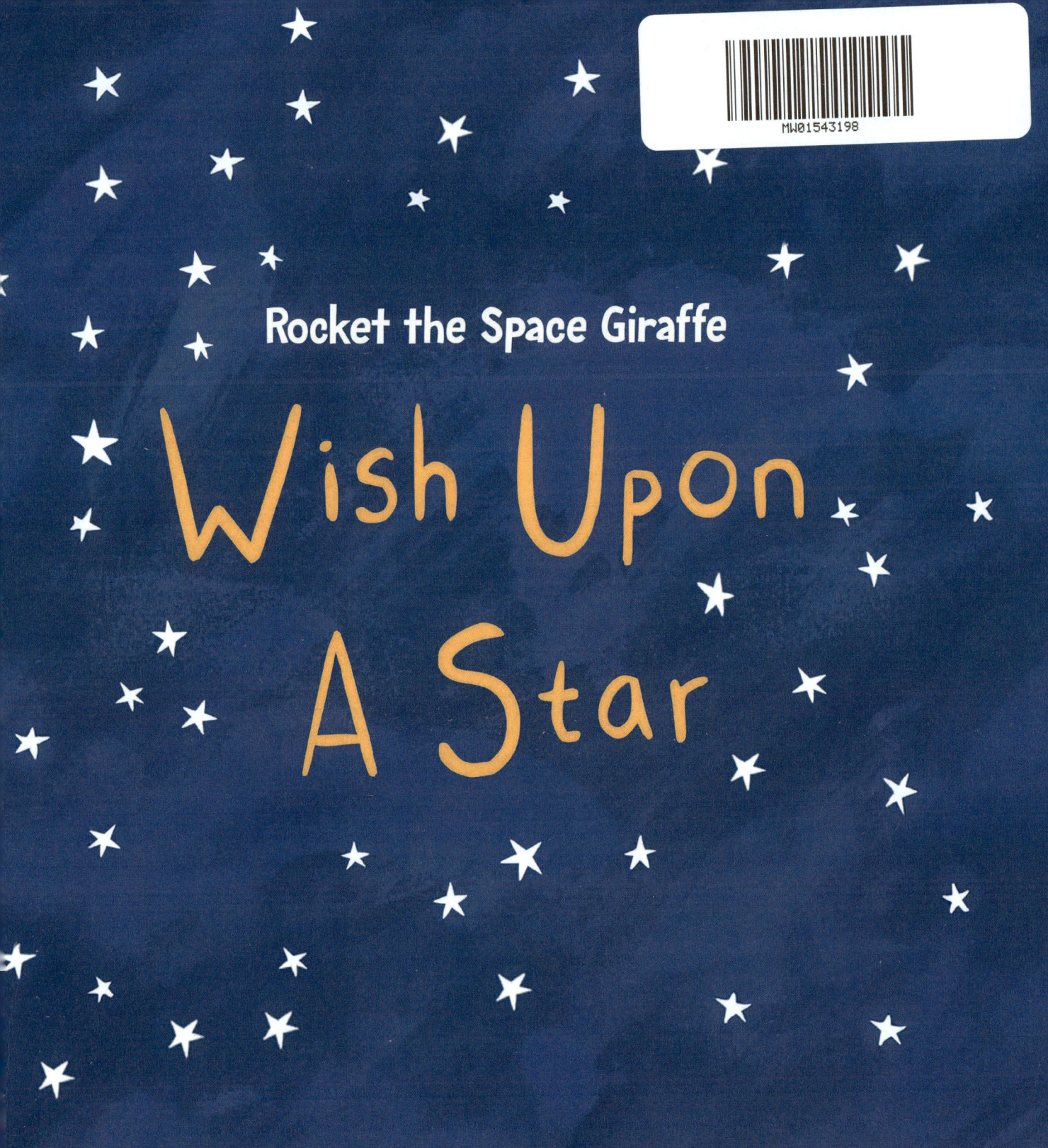

Rocket the Space Giraffe

Wish Upon A Star

© 2023 Donkey Friends, LLC

Brownsville, Texas 78520

or to Suzanne Shepard, c/o Gladys Porter Zoo, 500 Ringgold Street,
selections from this book, write to suzanne@suzanneshepard.com
permission. For information regarding permission to reproduce
mechanical, photocopying, recording, or otherwise, without written
system, or transmitted in any form or by any means, electronic,
No part of this publication may be reproduced, stored in a retrieval

Alejandra Rodriguez; Darlene Campbell; Sergio Garcia; Patricia Scanlan; and Anna Smith
Walter DuPree; Vanessa Cavazos; Dr. Deborah Carboni; Tony Peña; Arianna Barrera;
Colette Adams, Gladys Porter Zoo Deputy Director; Cynthia Garza Galvan;
Dr. Patrick Burchfield, Gladys Porter Zoo Director;

Credit page © Jafree, Adobe Stock
(Left page photo): Arianna Barrera; (Right page photos): Patricia Scanlan
"Come Visit the Real Rocket & Cosmo";
Photographs courtesy of Gladys Porter Zoo and the following:

Cynthia Garza Galvan, Gladys Porter Zoo Marketing Director and Editor

Tony Peña, Design and Layout Editor

Tilia Rand-Bell for Illustrations

Special thanks to the following:

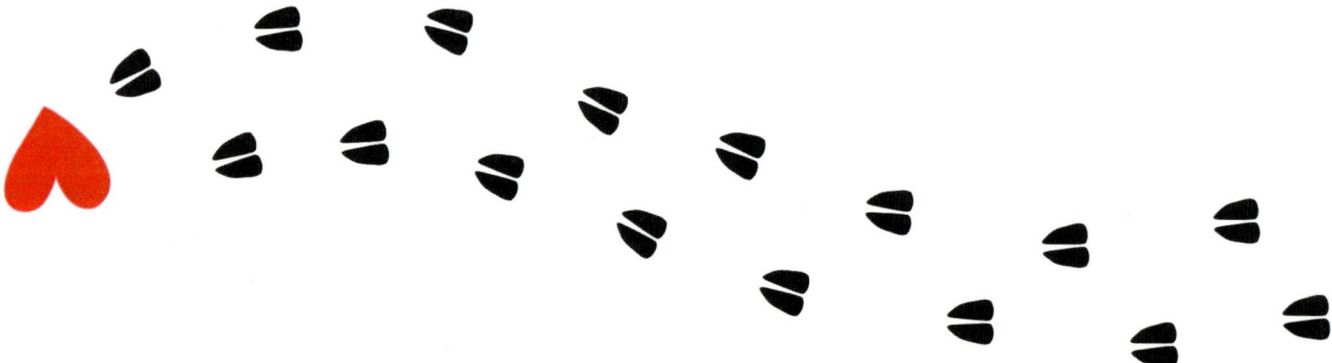

May your life be filled with beautiful stories.

—*Rocket*

Rocket the Space Giraffe

Wish Upon A Star

I wish I could fly to the moon.

In our rocket, we'll be there real soon.

We'll dance in the light . . .

. . . And then fly a kite.

I wish I could fly to the moon.

I wish I could swing on a star.
Fly high above and go far.

With so much starlight,
It sure will be bright.

I wish I could swing on a star.

I wish I could skate Saturn's rings.

We'll glide just as if we had wings.

We'll jump . . .

And then spin . . .

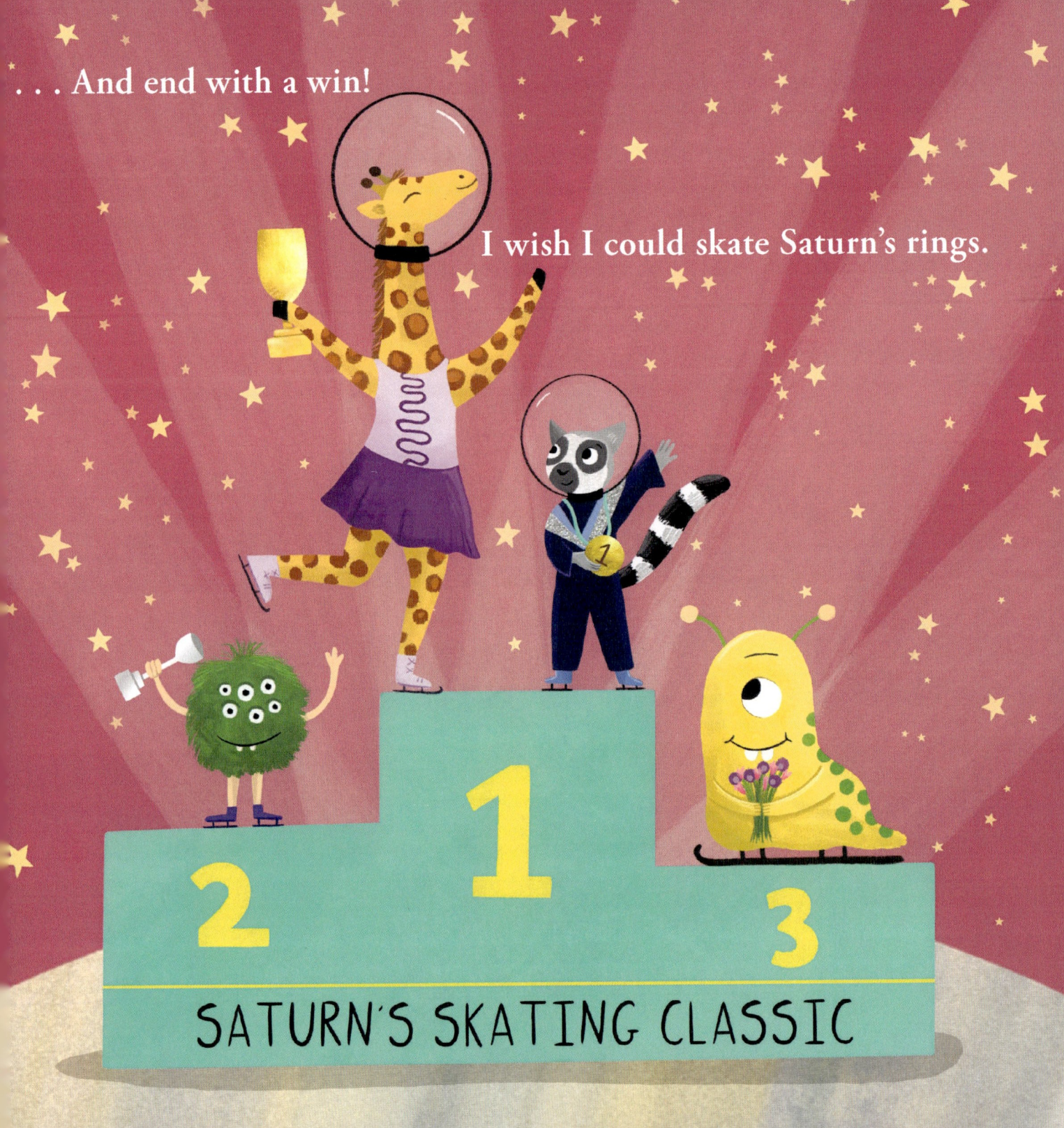

I wish I could race 'round the sun.
It really would be so much fun.

At the high speed of light . . .
. . . With no end in sight.

I wish I could race 'round the sun.

I wish I could see Mercury.
What a wonderful treat that would be.

In daytime it's hot . . .

. . . At night it is not.

I wish I could see Mercury.

I wish I could land on Mars.
With a bag full of chocolate bars.

If there's a Martian in sight...

...We'll give him a bite.

I wish I could land on Mars.

I wish upon a star just for you.
That all of your dreams will come true.

With love in your heart,
We're never apart.

I wish upon a star just for you.

COSMO

I am a ring-tailed lemur

HOME PLANET: Earth 🌍

When I Grow Up I Want To Be An Astronaut And A Painter.

My best friend is Rocket.

My birthday is July 12th

BE SURE TO FOLLOW US...

ROCKETTHESPACEGIRAFFE.COM
INSTAGRAM/@ROCKETTHESPACEGIRAFFE
GPZ.ORG
@GLADYSPORTERZOO

#ROCKETTHESPACEGIRAFFE

OR VISIT US...

GLADYS PORTER ZOO
500 E RINGGOLD ST
BROWNSVILLE, TX 78520

The Gladys Porter Zoo is a visitor-oriented zoological and botanical park, dedicated to the preservation of nature through education, conservation, healthy outdoor recreation and research. The Gladys Porter Zoo opened to the public on September 3, 1971. The facility was completely planned, built, stocked, equipped and then given to the City of Brownsville by the Earl C. Sams Foundation.

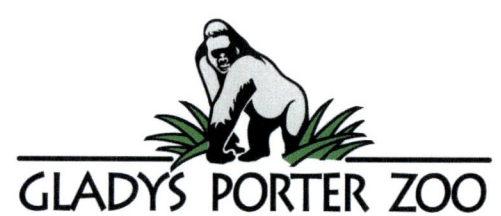

Suzanne Schwarz Shepard is the Past President of the Valley Zoological Society for Gladys Porter Zoo. She received a law degree from Baylor Law School and an LL.M. in International & Comparative Law from Georgetown Law Center. She lives in Harlingen, Texas with her husband Stephen, her mom Linda, five dogs, three cats, and three donkeys.

Her hope is that this book shares her love and affection for Rocket and the Gladys Porter Zoo and also highlights the importance of wildlife conservation.

Tilia Rand-Bell is an illustrator from Bristol, UK who works on many colorful books all over the world. Represented by the Bright Agency, she has several years' experience in creating and producing a range of unique and vibrant illustrations for children's markets and commercial businesses. Tilia has a huge passion for the environment and equality which comes across in her work.

When she's not drawing, she spends her time daydreaming about new places to travel, finding new places to eat, or playing with her rescue dog Disco.

Rocket and her friends wish you were here!

Be sure and also read her first adventure *Rocket the Space Giraffe*.

See you soon!

Made in the USA
Las Vegas, NV
30 November 2023